Theatre and Cabaret Comedy Songs

ISBN 978-1-4950-7268-0

HAL•LEONARD®
7777 W. Bluemound Rd. P.O. Box 13819 Milwaukee, WI 53213

Contents

ALONE

from *Young Frankenstein*

Music and Lyrics by
Mel Brooks

E♭6
me!
N.C.
Not dry e-nough! A - lone,
F♯m7(add4)
B7
here I am on my own.
E6
Fdim7
Cham -
F♯m7(add4)
pagne and foie gras, just
B7sus
twen - ty - two
B7
gar - çons and
E6
moi.
N.C.
Not dry e-nough! I'm so lost with-out you,
Am6/E
3

B7/E E Fdim7
life does-n't seem right. Al-though it's
F♯m7 N.C. Am6 N.C. E6 Fdim7
Pe-trus they're pour-ing, I find it all bor-ing. I need you to get through the
B7 G7 N.C. G+ C6
night. Too dry! A-lone,
Dm7 Dm7/G Em7♭5 A7 G♯7 A7
I'm so freak-in' a-lone. Danc-ing 'til
f

C♯dim7/D Dm E7 Am
half - past three, just twen - ty - two play - boys and me.
D9 Fm6 C6/G Fm6/G
Keep your ga - la pre - mieres, they bore me to tears. I
mf
C6/G Fm6/G C6/G
al - ways feel blue at a fan - cy to - do. Who needs e - la - tion, de -
cresc.
E7 Am Am/G D7 Fm6 N.C.
rall.
light - ful sen - sa - tion. I don't want fun, I want you! But I'm
rall.

G7
G7♭9
Dm7/G
C♯7
a tempo
fly - ing so - lo 'cause I'm so, oh, so a -
f
a tempo
C6
B♭9
C6
lone, a - lone,
Fm6
N.C.
Più mosso, in 2
C6
a - lone!
N.C./G
D♭9♯11
C

ALTO'S LAMENT

Lyrics by Marcy Heisler
Music by Zina Goldrich

Fmaj7 C/E Dm7 Cmaj7 Bm7♭5
tried to pick me out from all the voic-es in the crowd, I'm cer-tain that you must have had a
Slightly faster
E7sus E7 A7sus A7 A7(no3)/D Dm/F
pro - ble.... My plight is quite fa-mil-iar to those who tread the boards at the
Em7♭5 A7sus A7 A7(no3)/D Dm F6/9 F♯dim7
Ne-der-land-er, Shu-bert and Ri - al-to. Al-though I've got a great high "C," the re-
C6/G A9 C6/D D9 F6/G G7♯5
ac-tion seems to be, "Wow. That's great, dear, but we need you sing-ing al-to." Please,
slow roll

Andante (♩ = 85)
C6 accel. poco a poco
Dm7(add4) G7 C6 B♭7♭5
give me a chance to sing mel - o - dy. Give me a crack at the
mf accel. poco a poco
(♩ = 144)
A7 G9/B Cm6 A7/C♯ F♯m7♭5 Fm6 C6/E A7
tune. I'm filled with cha-grin ev - 'ry time I be-gin, "By the
D9 F/G G7 C(add2) E7 Am(add2) Am
light of the sil-ver-y moon." Just one lit-tle shot at the
F9 Am(add2) Am C6/D D9
mel - o - dy. Give me a mo - ment to shine. I'm

F♯m7♭5 Fm6 C6/E A♭7/E♭ Dm7 F/G G7 C Gm7 C7
sick of, "Can't help lov-in' that man of mine." Just
F(add2) F♯dim7 C6/G B♭/C C7 F(add2) F♯dim7
look at "O - kla - ho - ma" for ex - am - ple. That rous-ing ti-tled num-ber of the
C6/G B♭/C C7 F(add2) F♯dim7 C6/G Am7
show. While ev - 'ry - one is sing-ing, "O - kla - ho - ma" I get,
cresc.
"The Sound of Music"
Dm7 G7 C6 A♭ E♭m/A♭ A♭7
rit.
"Sky - y - y - y - y - y - y - y. Yo - ho!" The
(Spoken:) And now a medley of my finer roles.
f
mf
rit.

(♩ = 112)
D♭6/9 D♭(add2) D♭ D♭dim7
hills are a-live with the sound of mu - sic.
ff
"Three Little Maids"
Faster (♩ = 116)
D A7/D D A7/D D
Three lit-tle maids from school are we, pert as a school-girl well can be, filled to the
mf
A7/D D Bm7 E7sus E7 A
brim with girl-ish glee - ee, three lit-tle maids from school.
"Memory" (♩. = 55)
N.C./F
f
B♭ Gm C7
Touch me, it's so eas-y to leave me!
molto legato

♩. = 𝅗𝅥. "I Feel Pretty"
F C7 C F C7 F
What mir - ror, where?
mf
C Em/B B7
Which? What? Where? Who? Who?
mp
Em D7 G9 G7
Who? Who? Such a pret - ty me!
f
A♭9 A♭7 A♭
molto rit.
Such a pret - ty me! Please!
molto rit.

Pullback
D♭maj9
accel. poco a poco
D♭6
E♭m7
A♭7
Pull a few strings for the mel - o - dy! Don't
ff
accel. poco a poco
D♭maj9
D♭6
C♭7♯11
B♭7
A♭(add2)/C
D♭m6
B♭7/D
(♩ = 144)
Gm7♭5
G♭m6
care if the so - lo is tee - ny. It would be nir - va - na, from
a tempo
Fm7
B♭7
E♭9
G♭/A♭
A♭7
heav - en such man - na, to sing some - thing oth - er than
D♭m
A♭7
D♭maj9
D♭6
"Swee - ney!" I'm down on my knees for a
mf
gliss
f

E♭m7 A♭7 D♭maj9 D♭6 D♭6/C B♭m A 7
mel - o - dy. I'm beg-ging with all of my might! Just
D♭/A♭ E♭/A♭ D♭/A♭ D♭ A♭/C
half a bar, and let this cho - rus
mp
B♭m F m E♭m7(add4) A♭7
poco rit.
molto rit.
girl be a star! To -
f
ff
poco rit.
molto rit. e cresc.
D♭7 A♭7 D♭
a tempo
night.
a tempo

ALWAYS A BRIDESMAID

from *I Love You, You're Perfect, Now Change*

Lyrics by Joe DiPietro
Music by Jimmy Roberts

Quasi tempo
Lilting Country/Western Waltz (♩ = 120)
B/F♯ E/G♯ B/F♯ E/F♯ G♯m7 F♯7/A♯ B E B F♯7/A♯
al-ways a brides-maid, nev - er a bride. For
B B7/D♯ E B/D♯ C♯m7 B
Cat - lin, I wore sat - in, which I looked real - ly fat in. Then a-
sim.
E B/D♯ B F♯
gain, you should have seen her man Ken; all those
B D♯m7♭5 E C♯7/E♯
cal - o-ries he logged up, till his ar-ter-ies clogged up; he

B/F♯ E/G♯ B/F♯ E/F♯ G♯m7 F♯7/A♯ B E B F♯/A♯
died on the couch watch - ing E S P N.
G♯m D♯m/F♯ C♯m/E B/D♯
Too man - y wed - dings, too man - y dress - es that
sim.
G♯m C♯7/E♯ F♯ G♯m Adim F♯/A♯
all make my hips look so wide. Not a
G♯m D♯m/F♯ C♯m/E E♯m7♭5
gown I'd re - use, dit - to the match - ing shoes;
sim.

B/F♯ E/G♯ B/F♯ E/F♯ G♯m7 F♯/A♯ B E B F♯7/A♯
al - ways a brides - maid, nev - er a bride. For
B B9/D♯ E B
(spoken)
(sung)
Ta - bi - tha, I wore taf - fe - ta; you should nev - er... peo - ple laugh at ya'. But I
E6 B/D♯ B F♯
had a hunch her mar - riage was doomed. The
B D♯m7♭5 E C♯7/E♯
groom tried to stroke me while we danced the Ho - key - Po - key; they di -
cresc.

B/F♯ E/F♯ G♯m7 F♯7/A♯ B G7
vorced be-fore the hon-ey-moon. Once my
C C9/E F C
gown was ve-lour-ish; made me look kind of whor-ish. But my
F C/E F6 C/E C G C
best friend, De-lor-es, was nev-er quite sane. She shot her new
C9/E F D7/F♯ C/G
(can be spoken)
(sung)
mis-ter, 'cause he bed-ded her sis-ter; he's not dead, but now he

F/G Am7 G7/B C F C G/B Am Em/G
walks like John Wayne. Too man - y wed - dings,
Dm/F C/E Am D7/F♯ G Am A♯dim
too man - y dress - es, that all make me look so thick - thighed.
G/B Am Em/G Dm/F F♯m7♭5
My friends can't as - sess a man, or a dress;
C/G F/A C/G F/G Am7 G7/B C F C G7/B
al - ways a brides - maid, nev - er a bride. When I
rit.
rit.

Ad Lib. (conversationally)
C Em7♭5 F C/E Dm7 C F C/E
look in my clos-et, there's a rain-bow de-pos-it of gowns so gro-tesque that I
mp colla voce
G7 Freely C rit. Dm/C C7 F
groan. All those hus-bands are gone, but those dress-es live
mf
rit.
f
mf
8vb
D7/F♯ A tempo C/G F/G Am7 G7/B C F C G/B
on; e-ven moths seem to leave them a-lone.
A little more expansive
Am Em/G Dm/F C/E Am
Too man-y wed-dings, too man-y mess-es, but at least I've hung

D7/F♯
G
Am
A♯dim
G/B
rit.
on to my pride. I've
rit.
Reflectively (Ad lib.)
Firmly
Am
Em/G
F6
D9
rit.
lived life a - lone, but the terms are my own:
mp
mf
rit.
Freely, with feeling
C/G
F/A
C/G
F/G
Am7
G7/B
al - ways a brides - maid, never a
"Thank you, Lord!"
8va
loco
mp
mf
A tempo
F
C/G
F/A
F
C/E
Dm7
C
rit.
(opt.)
bride.
a tempo
rit.
f

BEWITCHED

from *Pal Joey*

Words by Lorenz Hart
Music by Richard Rodgers

Late - ly I've not slept a wink Since this half - pint im - i - ta - tion
rall.
a tempo
Put me on the blink. I'm wild a - gain! Be -
Seen a lot; I
Sweet a - gain, Pe -
rall.
p a tempo
guiled a - gain! A sim - per - ing, whim - per - ing child a - gain. Be -
mean a lot! But now I'm like sweet sev - en - teen a lot. Be -
tite a - gain, And on my pro - ver - bi - al seat a - gain. Be -
witched, both - ered and be - wil - dered am I.
witched, both - ered and be - wil - dered am I.
witched, both - ered and be - wil - dered am I.
f
p

Could - n't sleep And would - n't sleep Un -
I'll sing to him Each spring to him And
What am I? Half shot am I. To
til I could sleep where I should - n't sleep. Be - witched, both - ered and be -
wor - ship the trou - sers that cling to him. Be - witched, both - ered and be -
think that he loves me, So hot am I. Be - witched, both - ered and be -
wil - dered am I.
wil - dered am I.
wil - dered am I.
Lost my heart, but what
When he talks He is
Though at first we said
of it? My mis - take, I a - gree.
seek - ing Words to get off his chest.
"No, sir." Now we're two lit - tle dears.
p
f
p
mf

He's a laugh, but I love it Be-cause the laugh's on me. A
Hor - i - zon - tal - ly speak - ing, He's at his ver - y best.
You might say we are clos - er Than Roe - buck is to Sears. I'm
pill he is, But still he is All wine and I'll keep him un -
Vexed a - gain, Per - plexed a - gain, Thank God I can be o - ver -
dumb a - gain, And numb a - gain, A rich, read - y, ripe lit - tle
til he is Be - witched, both - ered and be - wil - dered like
sexed a - gain. Be - witched, both - ered and be - wil - dered am
plum a - gain. Be - witched, both - ered and be - wil - dered am
1, 2
me.
I.
3
rall.
I.
mf
rall.
8va
f
p

DANCE: TEN; LOOKS: THREE

from *A Chorus Line*

Music by Marvin Hamlisch
Lyric by Edward Kleban

G♭7
B♭m
looks: three,” is like to die! Left the thea - tre and
G♭maj7
E♭m9
F7
B♭m
G♭
called the doc - tor for my ap-point - ment to buy... tits and
Fm7
B♭m7
E♭m7(add11)
A♭7♭9
Cdim7/D♭
D♭6
ass. Bought my - self a fan - cy pair.
E♭m7(add11)
A♭7
Cdim7/D♭
D♭6
E♭9
A9♭5
Tight - ened up the der - ri - ère. Did the nose with it.

Ab13 Ddim7 Eb m7 Ab7 Db
All that goes with it. Tits and ass!
Ebm7(add11) Ab7 Dbmaj7#5 Bb7 Ebm7 Ab7
Had the bin - go - bon - gos done. Sud - den - ly I'm
Db Eb9 Db/F Gbm(maj7) Gm7b5
get - ting nash' nal tours!
Ebm9 Ab7 Fm7 Bbm7 Gb Fm F7b5 Bb7
Tits and ass won't get you jobs un -
p

E♭9
A♭7(add13)
D♭
less they're yours!
G♭9
F7
Did - n't cost a for - tune, neith-er. Did - n't hurt my sex life, eith - er.
f
mp
B♭m
Flat and sas - sy, I would get the strays and los - ers.
mf
G♭7
F7
E♭(add2)/G F7/A
Beg - gars real - ly can't be choos - ers. That ain't it, kid. That ain't it, kid.

Bbm
Gb(#11)(no3rd) Gb7
Fixed the chas - sis. "How do you do!"
Bbm
F7
Bbm
Life turned in - to an end - less med - ley of "Gee, it had to be you." Why?
p
Gb
Fm7
Bbm7
Ebm7(add11)
Ab7b9
Cdim7/Db
Db6
Tits and ass! Where the cup - board once was bare,
3
Ebm7(add11)
Ab7
Cdim7/Db
Db6
Eb9
A9b5
Ab13
Ddim7
now you knock and some - one's there. You have got 'em, hey. Top to bot - tom. Hey,

Ebm7 Ab7 Db Ebm7(add11) Ab7 Dbmaj7#5 Bb7
it's a gas! Just a dash of sil - i - cone.
Ebm7 Ab7 Db(b5) Db Eb9
Shake your new ma - ra - cas and you're fine!
Ebm9 Ab7 Fm7 Bbm7 Gb Fm F7b5 Bb7
Tits and ass can change your life. They
p
Eb9 Ab7(add13) Db F7
sure changed mine!

Slower
Bbm6 Bbm Bbm/Ab Gb7
Have it all done. Hon-ey, take my word.
3
Bbm Bbm/Ab Gbmaj7 Bbm/F Ebm9 Bbm/F F7
Grab a cab, c' mon. See the wiz - ard on Park and Sev - en - ty -
In 4
Bbm Bb7 Ebm7 Ab Dbmaj7 Ddim7
third for tits and ass.
Ebm7 Ab7 Db Ddim7 Ebm7 Ab9
Or-ches-tra and bal - co - ny, what they want is

Tempo I
Db
Eb9
A7#5 Gbmaj7/Ab
Ddim7
what cha see.
Keep the best of you.
Do the rest of you.
f
Ebm7
Ab7
Dbmaj7
Ddim7
Ebm7
Ab7
Pits, or class.
I have nev - er
Dbmaj7
Ddim7
Ebm7
Ab7
Db
seen it fail.
Deb - u - tante or chor - us girl or
Eb7
Bbm7/F
Gbdim7
E7/G
wife.

Ebm7/Ab
Ab6
Ebm7/Ab
Ab6
Tits and ass, yes, tits and
Ebm
ass have changed
Ab7
Db
Db/Cb
my
life!
ff
Db/A
Db/Ab
Db
sfz
8vb

GETTING MARRIED TODAY

from *Company*

Music and Lyrics by
Stephen Sondheim

This ensemble has been adapted as a solo for this edition with the composer's blessing.

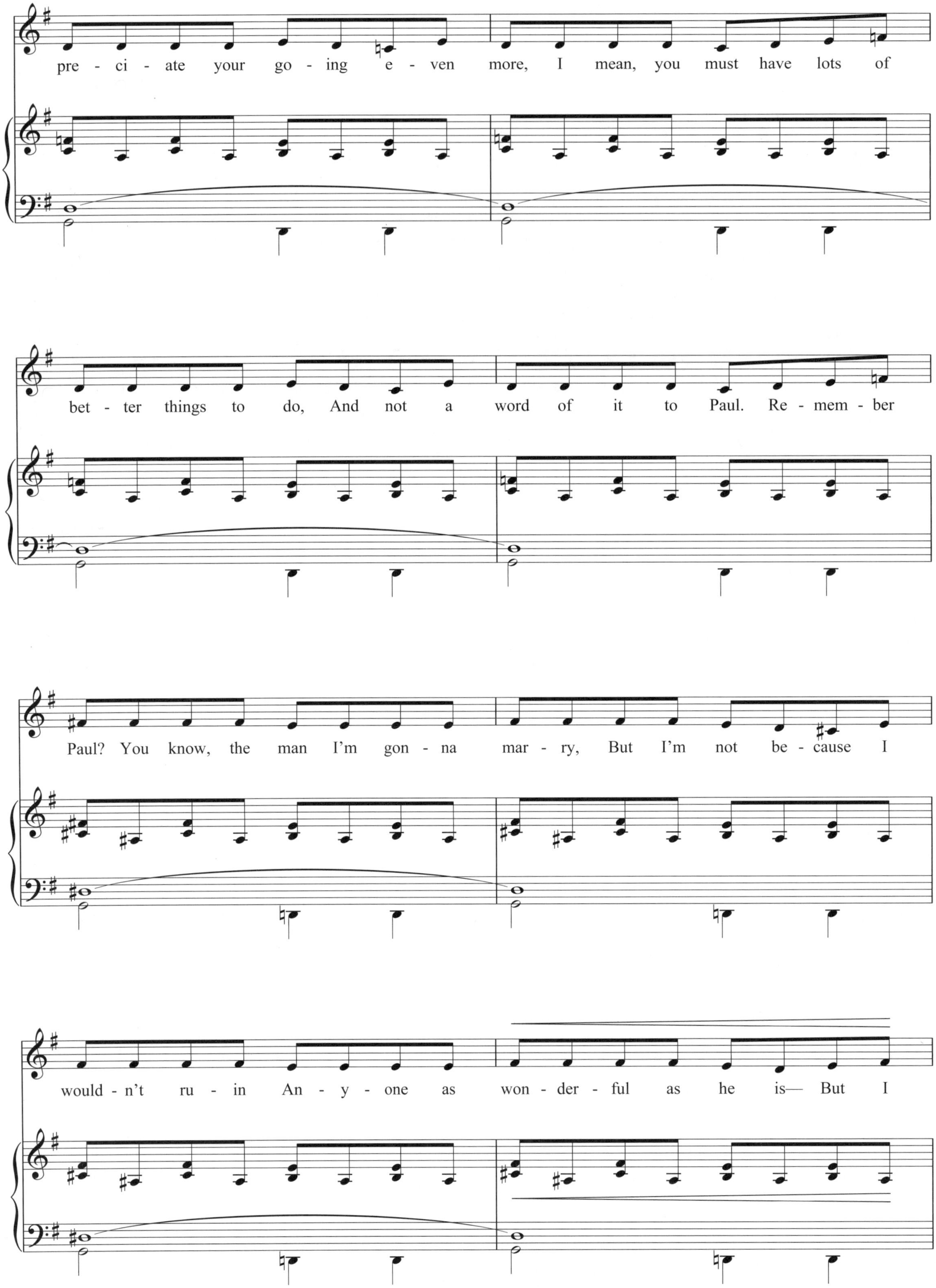
pre - ci - ate your go - ing e - ven more, I mean, you must have lots of
bet - ter things to do, And not a word of it to Paul. Re - mem - ber
Paul? You know, the man I'm gon - na mar - ry, But I'm not be - cause I
would - n't ru - in An - y - one as won - der - ful as he is— But I

mf
thank you all For the gifts and the flow-ers. Thank you all, Now it's
mf
back to the show-ers. Don't tell Paul, But I'm not get-ting mar-ried to-
day.
Lis-ten, ev-'ry-bod-y, Look, I don't know what you're wait-ing for. A

wed - ding, what's a wed - ding? It's a pre - his - tor - ic rit - u - al Where
ev - 'ry - bod - y prom - is - es fi - del - i - ty for - ev - er, Which is
may - be the most hor - ri - fy - ing word I ev - er heard, And which is
fol - lowed by a hon - ey - moon Where sud - den - ly he'll re - a - lize He's
(♮)
(♮)

mf
sad-dled with a nut and want to kill me, which he should. So lis-ten, Thanks a bunch, But I'm
mf
not get-ting mar-ried. Go have lunch 'Cause I'm not get-ting mar-ried.
f
You've been grand, But I'm not get-ting mar-ried. Don't just stand There, I'm
f
not get-ting mar-ried! And don't tell Paul, But I'm not get-ting mar-ried to-

day. Go! Can't you
go? Why is no - Bod - y lis - ten - ing? Good -
bye! Go and cry At an - oth - er per - son's
wake. If you're quick, For a kick, You could

pick Up a christ - en - ing, But please, On my
knees, There's a hu - man life at stake!
Lis - ten, ev - 'ry - bod - y, I'm a - fraid you did - n't hear, Or do you
want to see a cra - zy la - dy Fall a - part in front of you? It

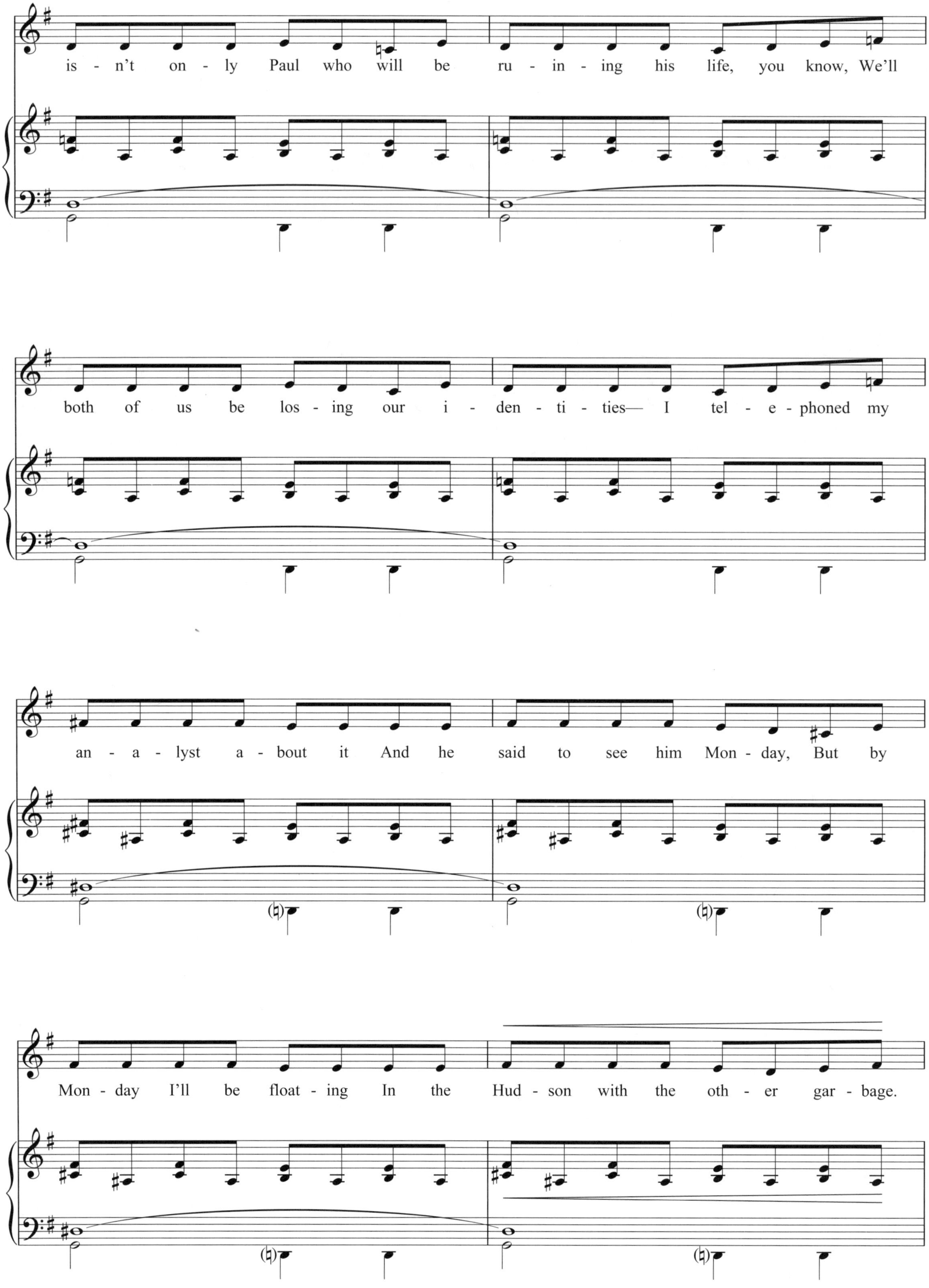
is - n't on - ly Paul who will be ru - in - ing his life, you know, We'll
both of us be los - ing our i - den - ti - ties— I tel - e - phoned my
an - a - lyst a - bout it And he said to see him Mon - day, But by
Mon - day I'll be float - ing In the Hud - son with the oth - er gar - bage.

mf
I'm not well, So I'm not get-ting mar-ried. You've been swell, But I'm
mf
not get-ting mar-ried. Clear the hall 'Cause I'm not get-ting mar-ried.
f
Thank you all, But I'm not get-ting mar-ried, And don't tell Paul, But I'm
f
not get-ting mar-ried to - day!

DON'T CALL ME TRAILER TRASH

from *Cowgirls*

Written by Mary Murfitt

Steadily

All the girls are skin - ny, and their hair is flat. Why would
pick - up truck with o - ver - sized tires makes me
G
C
G
I want to look like that? I like the fash - ion don'ts
weak in the knees and sets my heart on fire. Cheese fries, wise guys,
C
G
and not the do's. I read the com - ics, and I
dem - o - li - tion der - by. Stir frys, nice guys
C
throw a - way the news. Cit - y folks laugh at my K - Mart clothes, but I
do noth - in' fer me. Nev - er cut out gour - met rec - i - pes, I pre -

G
C
got my own style and I got my own nose.
fer the cui - sine at the Tas - ty Freeze.
F
C
G
12 - Step pro - grams make me yawn, but I could two - step
I like a car with lots of chrome. I can make art out of
C
F
C
all night long. Pink fla - min - gos on my lawn,
sty - ro - foam. I ain't got no cel - lu - lar phone,
N.C.
C
F
but don't call me trail - er trash. I live
Footstomp

G
1
C
in a mo - bile home.
2
C
F
home. Don't call me trail - er trash.
G N.C.
C
I live in a mo - bile home.
G
C
G
C

THE GIRL IN 14G

Music by Jeanine Tesori
Lyrics by Dick Scanlan

Pets are banned, par-ties too, and no so-li-ci-
mf
ta-tions. Win-dow seat with gar-den view.
No swing
A per-fect nook to read a book. I'm lost in my Jane Aus-ten when I
L.H.
mp
decresc. poco a poco
À la "Tristan" (no swing)
hear: "Ah, ah."
5
ff

Tempo I (Swing)
Say it is - n't so. Not the flat be -
sub. p
low. From an op - 'ra wan - na be___ in
Thir - teen "G,"___ a mat - i - nee of some can - ta - ta, Wag-ner's Ring and Tra - vi - a - ta.
mp
Faster, à la "Magic Flute" (no swing)
"Ah, ah, ah, ah, ah, ah, ah, ah, ah, ah, ah, ah, ah, ah, ah, ah, ah, ah, ah, ah, ah, ah, ah,
ff mf

À la "Tristan"
ah, ah, ah, ah, ah, ah, ah, ah,
ah,
f
Ped.
À la "Magic Flute"
tr
ah, ah, ah, ah, ah,
ah, ah, ah, ah, ah,
ah, ah, ah, ah, ah, ah, ah, ah,
mf
Tempo I (Swing)
ah, ah, ah, ah."
fff
sub. p

My first night in Four-teen "G." I'll put up with Puc -
ci - ni. Brew my - self a cup of tea.
sim.
Cro - chet un - til she's fi - ni. Half past eight,
mf
not a peep ex - cept the clock tick tock - in'.

No swing
Now I lay me down to sleep.
A com - fy bed
L.H.
mp
to rest my head. A stretch, a yawn; I'm al - most gone, then
rit. e dim.
R.H.
Fast Jazz, à la Ella Fitzgerald (Swing)
f
"Doo - wee - zwah doo -
tah - dup - doo spee - di - lee dee - floy - doy bee - blip,

opt.
naa - naa - naa - naa - naa - naa - naa - naa - naa - naa - naa - naa, woo - weeee.
Tempo I
Now the girl up - stairs wakes me un - a - wares.
sub. p
Blow - in' down from Fif - teen "G" her
rev - eil - le. She's scat - tin' like her name is El - la. Guess who an - swers a cap - pel - la.
mp
lightly

Fast Jazz ("Ella")
Operatic
"Zoot doo doot floy doy."
"Ah."
f
mf molto legato
Fast Jazz ("Ella")
Operatic
"Zoot doo doot floy dee doy."
"Ah."
f
mf molto legato
Somewhat freely
I'm not one to raise my voice, make a fuss or speak my mind, but
sub. mp
might I quer - y... Would you mind if... Could you kind - ly... stop!
poco accel.
pp
ppp
colla voce

Fast March
staccato
cresc. poco a poco
"That felt good" Stop!
f
molto rit.
Broad Swing
ff
Thir - teen, Fif - teen,
Four-teen "G." A most un - like - ly tri - o.

Operatic
Not quite three - part har - mo - ny.
All day, all night we're sing - in':
Fast Jazz
"Zoot doo doot floy doy a zee bop boo doo
boy ta boy."
"Stop!"
"Ah.

Broad swing
Ah." Had my fill
of peace and qui - et. Shout out loud. I've
changed my di - et, all be - cause of Four - teen "G!"
rit.

GOOCH'S SONG

from *Mame*

Music and Lyrics by
Jerry Herman

Moderately slow 2
al - tered the drape of a drop of my bod - ice And
soft - ened the shape of my brow.
I fol - lowed di - rec - tions, And made some con - nec - tions, But
what do I do now?
Who'd
R. H.

think this Miss Prim would Have o - pened a win - dow As
far as her whim would al - low? And
who would sup - pose it Was so hard to close it, Oh,
what do I do now? I

pol - ished and pow - dered and puffed my - self. If
life is a ban - quet I stuffed my - self. I
had my mis - giv - ings, But went on a field trip To
R. H.
find out what liv - ing's a - bout. My

thanks for the train-ing Now I'm not com-plain-ing, But
you left some-thing out!
Freely
In-stead of
wan-d'ring on with my lone re-morse, I have come back home to com-plete the course. Oh,
Tempo I°
What do I do---

Spoken:
Mrs. Burnside,
(sung)
I trav-eled to hell in my new ven-eer, And
look what I got as a sou-ven-ir! But still I'll de-
fend you as guide and in-struct-or. Would I rec-om-mend you? And
how! Al-though I was leer-y, I
R. H.
3

thrived on your theo-ry That life can be a wow!
Freely
You said there's noth-ing wrong with a harm-less smooch, So I'm gon-na call him
Tempo I°
Burn-side Gooch! Oh, what do I do
(opt.)
now?
ff
sfz

THE HISTORY OF WRONG GUYS

from the Broadway Musical *Kinky Boots*

Words and Music by
Cynthia Lauper

B♭5
Wom-en have been mak-ing bad choic - es
F/A
A♭5
since the be -
E♭5
gin - ning of time.
B♭5
Are you gon - na be an - oth - er
F/A
one of mine?
A♭5
Uhn- ohw.
E♭5
B♭5
Used to think you were from out-er
F/A
space.
A♭5
Who's this bright eyed guy
E♭5
in your place?
B♭5
You're kind of cute.

F/A
Ab5
Eb5
when you're not so shy. Uhn - ohw.
Bb5
F/A
Ab5
I've been here be-fore. Have I come back for more? An-oth-er chap-ter in the
mf
Eb5
Bb5
F/A
his-to-ry of wrong guys. You used to be so "eh," a limp lack-lus-ter bore.
Ab5
Eb5
Bb5
But now you're chang ing in-to some one I just can't ig-nore Char - lie,
f

F
C5
F
B♭5
hon - est - ly,
I've been hurt
F
C5
like this be - fore.
B♭5
F
C5
Is there rea - ly more to you than what I al - ways thought?
F
B♭5
F
How can you sur - prise me an - y - more,

-ore,
-ore,
-ore?
Bb5
F/A
Ab5
Eb5
(Spoken:) He's got a girlfriend, you flake. Why are they only nice when they're unavailable?
subito mp
Bb5
F/A
Ab5
Don't wan-na be an-oth-er star crossed lov - er. We all know
Eb5
Bb5
F/A
how that ends. I'm bet-ter off with-out him, we're bet-ter off as friends.

A♭5
E♭5
B♭5
F/A
Uhn-ohw.
But I've been here be-fore.
Have I come back for more?
mf
A♭5
E♭5
B♭5
An-oth-er chap-ter in the his-to-ry of wrong guys.
Yes-ter-day no spark,
F/A
A♭5
E♭5
no heart ach-ing al-lure.
But to-day I'm feel-ing some-thing I just can't ig-nore
B♭5
F
E♭5
F
Char - lie,
hon - est - ly,
f

B♭5
F
C5
I've been hurt like this be - fore. -ore, -ore,
-ore.
B♭5
F
The his-to-ry of wrong guys. Chap-ter
f
C5
D5
E5
one, he's a bum. Two: he's not in - to you. Three: he's a sleaze.
subito p cresc. poco a poco
F5
G5
A5
Four: loves the girl next door. Five: Loves the boy next door. Six: don't love you no more,

makes you in - se - cure, makes you so un - sure, is so im - ma - ture, loves his moth - er more,
f
colla voce
N.C.
or... has a girl-friend named Ni - co - la. Er...
a tempo
a tempo
drums
B♭5
F
C5
Char - lie,
hon - est - ly,
ff
F
B♭5
F
I've been hurt like this be -

C5
fore.
B♭5
I can see there's more
F
to you
than what
C5
I al-ways
F
thought.
B♭5
But I won't be
F
burned an - y - more.
C5
-ore,
-ore,
-ore
N.C.
(Spoken:)
I've been executized.
a tempo
F5
a tempo
ff

I AM PLAYING ME

from *[title of show]*

Words and Music by
Jeff Bowen

D7♭9 N.C. D7 G13 C
Stuck in a show where I am play - ing me.
G C G+
I'm trapped in a hole,
C G+ F7 N.C. F7
no - where to go with my role. Strain - in' my neck for an ex -
G N.C. G Em7/A A7
- it that sets me free.
3
3

D7♭9 N.C. D7 G13 C
Stuck in a role where I am play - ing me.
E7 Am
I in - sist I could make 'em mis - ty
F7 G Am
hid - in' in - side Miss An - na Christ - ie. And Lord knows I could
F7 E7
raise the roof play - in' the maid that goofs in Tar - tuffe. And I could

Am
car - ry on the his - to - ry of play - in' a dude in the
F7 N.C. F7 E7
ti - tle role of The Mys - ter - y of Ed - win Drood.
F7 E7 G13
Not a
C G+ C N.C.
chance for my ca - reer to ad - vance and there's no straight guys here for

G+ N.C. F7 G
me to ro-mance. I guess I'll swal-low my pride and make the best of the rest of this spree!
Em7 A7♭9 F7
Stuck in a show where
N.C. C/G N.C. C/G Gsus(add2) G C C/B♭
I am play - ing me!
C/A C/A♭ C/G C
8va
8vb

I DON'T KNOW WHAT I'D DO WITHOUT YOU

from *A Gentleman's Guide to Love and Murder*

Music by Steven Lutvak
Lyrics by Robert L. Freedman
and Steven Lutvak

B7 B7/D♯ Em B7 Em
Vio - let? No, at - tar of ros - es, I think. Look,
A7 A7/C♯ A7/A G(add2)/B A7/C♯ D
you brought me choc - 'lates! Oh, no, I don't dare. Do
G7 G7/B C C/G
you hate these ear - rings? The truth; don't be kind. I don't
B7 B7/D♯ Em B7 Em
mind, be - cause I hate them too.

E♭7
G/D
No, no, no, don't squeeze. Mon - ty, you're a tease.
Meno Mosso
F♯m7♭5
B7
Em
Cm6/E♭
Oh, Mon - ty, look, my shoe! I don't
A Tempo
G/D
Am7/D
D7
G
know what I'd do with - out you!
Dm7
G7
C6
I have nev - er met an - oth - er man who's half as dear as you. You're so

Dm7 G7 C
clev - er too. And you make me laugh more than an - y - bod - y.
Dm7 G7 C C/G
Why are oth - er men so drear - y, Mon - ty, and so dead - ly dull? No one
F♯m7♭5 F7♭5 Bm/E A9
rit.
holds a con - ver - sa - tion half as beau - ti - f'lly as
rit.
Slowly
A Tempo
D9 G C C/G
you! You have-n't said a word a-bout my dress! You're a brute!

G7 G7/B C B7
See how it moves when I turn? Two - three - one - two. It's a bit much for
B7/D♯ Em B Em E♭7
Clap-ham, but nev - er - the - less. May-be just a bite.
G/D F♯m7♭5 B7 Fdim
rit.
Just to be po - lite. Mon - ty, that's too tight. Mon - ty, that's just
Slowly
E7 F♯m7♭5 B7 Em Cm6
right. Oh, what I put you through! I don't

G/D
Am7/D
G/D
accel. poco a poco
a tempo
know what I'd do, I do not have a
accel. poco a poco
a tempo
Cm6
G/D
clue, I don't know what I'd
Am/D
G
Am7
B♭dim7
do with - out you!
f
G/B
Am7
D7
G
Don't you just love me in pink?
p
f

I NEVER DO ANYTHING TWICE

from *The Seven Percent Solution*

Words and Music by
Stephen Sondheim

vis - it - ed my cham - bers One eve - ning ve - ry late, In
eve - ning that we shared Was me - tic - u - lous - ly planned: He
made a pro - po - si - tion (Which I found rath - er sweet) And
tan - dem with a husk - y St. Ber - nard. At
took the most ex - traor - di - na - ry pains. He
hand - ed me a ham - mer and some nails. In
first I was as - ton - ished, And tears came to my eyes, But
trem - bled with ex - cite - ment, His cheeks were quite a - glow. And
time we lay con - tent - ed, And he be - gan a - gain By
la - ter when I asked him to re - sume, He
af - ter - wards he cried to me, "En - core!" He
fin - ger - ing the beads a - round our waists. I

said, to my sur - prise, "My dear, it is - n't wise. Where
plead - ed with me so To have a - noth - er go, I
whis - pered to him then, "We'll have to say A - men," For
rit.
love is con - cerned, One must fresh - en the bloom.
mur - mured car - ess - ing - ly, "What - ev - er for?
I had de - vel - oped more cath - o - lic tastes.
rit.
a tempo
(Each Chorus, a little brighter, more strict rhythm)
Once, yes, once for a lark. Twice,
Once, yes, once for a lark. Twice,
Once, yes, once for a lark. Twice,
a tempo
though, los - es the spark. One must
though, los - es the spark. Once, yes,
though, los - es the spark. As I

nev - er de - ny it, But af - ter you try it You
once is de - li - cious, But twice would be vi - cious, Or
said to the Ab - bot, "I'll get in the ha - bit, But
rit.
a tempo
va - ry the di - et." Said my
just re - pe - ti - tious. Some - one's
not in the ha - bit." You've my
rit.
a tempo
hand - some young Guard, "Yes, I
bound to be scarred— Yes, I
high - est re - gard, And I
know that it's hard. Still, no mat - ter how
know that it's hard. Still, no mat - ter the
know that it's hard— Still, no mat - ter the

nice, I nev - er do an - y - thing twice."
price, I nev - er do an - y - thing twice."
vice, I nev - er do an - y - thing twice."
1, 2
3
Mmm - mmm mmm mmm mmm - mmm.
Mmm - mmm mmm mmm mmm - mmm.
2. I
3. And
cresc.
Once, yes, once can be nice: Love
re - qui - res some spice. If you've

some - thing in view, Some - thing to do To - tal - ly
new, I'll be there in a trice! But I
ten.
nev - er do an - y - thing twice— Ex - cept— No, I
ten.
nev - er do an - y - thing twice.

I WANT THEM... (BALD)

Lyrics by Marcy Heisler
Music by Zina Goldrich

Em7 Am7 C/D D7
breed - ing, but the sing - u - lar trait that I love in a mate, is a
8va
Tango-like (♩ = 120)
Dm7 G7sus E7♯5 Am9
rit.
hair - line that's re - ced - ing... I want them bald,
rit.
f
Gm7 C13 F6/9
tall, dark, hand - some, and bald.
Bm7♭5 Bm7♭5/E E7
Keep your jock, and keep your rock star;

*Backup vocals are optional.

Amaj9
F♯m9
love when he goes for a hair - cut, and I mean...
f
Bm9
E13
E13/D
a hair - cut, (A hair - cut) and he
C♯m9
F♯m9
comes home re - laxed, with that self - as - sured sat - is - fied
Bm9
E13
flair. (flair!) He says,
mf

C♯m7♭5
F♯7
"Hon', like the style?" And I give a soft smile,
8va
mp
mf
Bm
as I gent - ly run my
cresc.
Bm(maj7)
Bm7
F7♯11
E7
fin - gers through his air. (He has no hair.) He's
(cresc.)
Am7
Gm7
C13
bald, (he is so bald) and I love him so
f

F6/9
Bm7♭5
bald. (love him so bald) Who needs tan - gles?
mf
Bm7♭5/E
E7
Bm7♭5
E7
Bm7♭5
E7
Am
Who needs gel? You can tell Jean Paul Da - vid to go to hell! And to
Amaj9
F♯m9
all you young men who are list - 'ning, who do the tou -
f
Bm9
E9
E9/D
pée thing, (tou - pée thing) and

C♯m9
F♯m9
make no mis - take, I as - sure you, we know who you
Bm9
E13
are, (who you are) and to
B♭maj7
Gm9
all you young men who do one piece real long, or that
Cm9
F13
spray thing: (that spray thing) just go

Dm7
Gm9
Fm11
au na - tu - rel', and be - lieve me, you'll shine like a star,
(shine like a star)
(shine like a star)
G7♯5(♯9)
'cause wom - en love
cresc.
Cm(add2)
B♭m9
E♭13
bald. (wom - en love bald) (Spoken): My ba - by will be
A♭maj9
bald. (Sung): (ba - by, be bald)

Dm7♭5
D7
I'm tel - ling you, don't be a fool,
Cm/G
Fm6
Cm/G
just take a tip from Sean and Yul. What could be more
Cm/G
A♭/G
G7
Cm(add2)
hot, more cool than bald.
(slide)
mf sub.
f
B♭m9
E♭13
A♭maj9
G7♯5(♯9)
Cm(maj9)
(Spoken): "Who loves ya, ba - by...?" (growl)

MY PARTY DRESS
from *Henry and Mudge*

Words and Music by Kait Kerrigan
and Brain Lowdermilk

E♭
A°/E♭
that was on my oth - er dress. John Mi-chael stole my birth-day cake and
mf a tempo
E♭/B♭
B+
Jen - na Walk - er tried to take my Crunch 'N' Munch. It was - n't fair. I
Cm
E♭/D♭
B♭7/D
E♭
B♭/F
E♭/G
rit.
grabbed the punch. I climbed a chair. But then I fell and punch went ev - 'ry -
rit.
B♭7/A♭
N.C.
where. On the floor. On my chair. On his shoes. In her
colla voce
mp

E♭
hair. But it was - n't on my par - ty dress. John
mp a tempo
F/A
F
Mi - chael once made fun of soc - cer, so I stuffed him in a lock - er.
sfz
B♭7
N.C.
B♭5
B♭5(maj7)
N.C.
I play soc - cer and I play the flute. I do art and Dis -
mp
colla voce
cov - ery Camp and tum - bling and tee - ball and I

E♭ B♭/E♭ E♭ F/E♭
a tempo
play pi - an - o ev-'ry night. My dad says I'm a prod - i - gy, but
mf a tempo
E♭/B♭
I think I would rath - er be the F - B - I or C - I - A, a
C♭+ A♭/C E♭ B♭7/F E♭/G B♭7/A♭ N.C.
rit.
se - cret spy who saves the day, and when I'm fin-ished sav - ing it I'll play "Ode to
rit. colla voce
accel.
Joy," "In - jun Joe," "Frè - re Ja - cques," "Al - le - gro," the
accel.

Cm7
accel.
B♭/D
E♭
E°7
Pach - el - bel "Can - on" and al - so this song I wrote:
f
accel. e. cresc
Ballet, in 1 (𝅗𝅥.= 72)
B♭
Am
Gm7
Ah - ah - ah. La - la - la - la - la. La - la - la - la -
mp sub.
C
F
F7
B♭
Am
la. La - la - la - la - la. It has words: "I'm a spy.
f
Gm7
N.C.
C
molto rit.
And it's real - ly fun. And I wear a cape. And..."
colla voce
mp
molto rit.
petering out

Tempo primo
E♭
A°/E♭
Do you like my par - ty dress? When I do pir - ou - ettes it rus - tles.
mf
N.C.
A°/E♭
N.C.
I buy all my clothes in Brus - sels.
B♭7
rall.
N.C.
Dad says that's where Brus - sels sprouts are from. I've toured Brus - sels, and
rall.
Par - is, and Vi - en - na, and this one time, we pre - tend - ed to go to

Rome but we went to Ice - land. And in Ice - land, my dad pre -
freely
3
(spoken) That was a secret.
sid - ed o-ver an in - ter - na - tion - al cor - p'rate trade_ hear - ing... Whoops. And we
E♭
a tempo
F7
saw the Rey - kja - vík Bal - let. My dance class is on Sat - ur - day. Miss
mf
a tempo
E♭/B♭
B+
Lau - ra and Miss Li - sa say I'm much more bright than I ap - pear. I

Cm Eb/Db Bb7/D Eb Bb/F Eb/G Bb7/Ab N.C.
rit.
chas - sé right. It's ver - y clear that I'll be in The Nut-crack - er next year as a
rit.
mp
Fm
accel.
mouse, then a sol - dier, then a can - dy cane or a
a tempo
accel. e. cresc
Bb7 Cm7 Bb/D
mar - zi - pan, then a Rus - sian or an an - gel, then a
Eb E°7 F+
molto rit.
Po - li - chi - nelle. Let me dance to this
molto rall.

G♭+
song 'cause I wrote it so well. It goes
r.h.
Ballet, in 1 (𝅗𝅥. = 72)
C♭
B♭m
"Ah - ah - ah. I will dance un-
f
A♭m7
D♭
G♭
G♭7
til I play all the parts in the great bal - let." Sing with me.
C♭
B♭m
"Ah - ah - ah." I will do a

A♭m
N.C.
D♭
turn.
And an - oth - er turn.
mp colla voce
N.C.
B♭m
a tempo
E♭7♯5
Moth - er says I'll quit. I will ne - ver quit. I will do a
mf a tempo
A♭m
D♭9
N.C.
B7
split.
And I guess that's it.
Oh and
Maestoso (♩ = 104)
E
one day when I'm pres - i - dent,
my
f

F♯
F♯m/A
bed - time will be ver - y late so I have time to leg - is - late the kinds
E/G♯
A maj7
A♯m7(♭5)
of laws I think are cool. I'll pass a clause to ban - ish school. And
B7
rit.
N.C.
freely
then all of the coun - tries that I rule will be
rit.
8vb
peace - ful, and hap - py, and
colla voce
p

B 9
com - fort-'ble, and sat - in,
Ballet, in 1 (𝅗𝅥.= 72)
F♯7
accel.
B 5/C♯
and frill - y, and
accel.
f
with pedal
B/D♯
E
pret - ty, and lac - y and
D°7
poco rit.
silk - y and per - fect and pink like my
poco rit.

freely
B/D♯
N.C.
pa
ah
ah-ah - ah - ah - ah -
cadenza
4
N.C./B♭
E♭m/B♭
B♭
ah...
My
par - ty
colla voce
Presto
8
N.C.
E♭
A°
E♭
B♭
dress!
f
12
E♭
B♭
E♭
B♭
E♭
B♭
E♭
8vb

LISTEN TO YOUR HEART

from *Young Frankenstein*

Music and Lyrics by
Mel Brooks

be a coup - le of dumb - bells, Dumb right from the
start. Lose your mind ’cause love is blind and
listen to your heart.
Let’s be stu - pid to -
geth - er. Not a thought in our head.
3
f

Bird - brains of a feath - er who'll fly right in - to
bed. Let's be to - tal - ly fool - ish, two
mf
nit - wits nev - er a - part. You'll find such bliss in the
slightly swinging
kiss - in' we're miss - in' so lis - ten, lis - ten to your
mp

heart. As ev - 'ry - bod - y knows, if it's
sex they're think - ing of, in - tel - lec - tu - als are in - ef - fec - tu - als when it
comes to mak - ing love. Nietz - sche al - ways said he
would - n't. Scho - pen - hau - er thought he should - n't. And
mf
mp
mp

as for E - man - u - el Kant, Ev - 'ry girl in town knew that
Kant could-n't. Let's be blith - er - ing
id - i - ots, sing - ing love's sweet song. We'll
blith - er ev - 'ry morn - ing and blith - er all night
rall.
mp
rall.

Meno mosso
long. Let's find things un - dis - cov - ered,
mf
don't re - sist Cu - pid's dart.
Soft & seductively
You'll find such joy just in
colla voce
be - ing a boy, so lis - ten,
lis - ten to your
p
heart.

MY NEW PHILOSOPHY

from *You're A Good Man, Charlie Brown*

Words and Music by
Andrew Lippa

SALLY: *Spoken (before the vamp): "Why are you telling me?"* (beat) *I like it.*

Moderately bright Swing, in 4

* *Original key: A Major*
The song is a duet for Sally and Schroeder. The composer created this solo edition for publication.

C6
Cm7
Cm6
Bm7
Sal - ly Brown, your grades are go - ing down." I could have
Bm7/E
E/B
B♭9♯11
Asus
F+/E♭
D
D7
told her my new phi - los - o - phy.
(as teacher) Miss B?
G D7/F♯
G D7/F♯
G D7/F♯
(as herself) I'm she.
(as teacher) Look see.
(as herself) A "D"?
(as teacher) A "D".
B♭7/D
N.C.
G7
Spoken (as herself): Well, why are you telling me?
And that's my new phi - los - o - phy!!
sfz
mf

C Db9 Dsus G7
Spoken: Why are you telling me? My new phi - los - o - phy! And like a
bus - y bee, each new phi - los - o - phy can fly from
G Am7 A#dim7 G/B Cmaj7
tree to tree and keep me mov - ing. When life's a
C6 Cm7 Cm6 Bm7
diz - zy maze, on al - ter - nat - ing days, I choose a
mf

Bm7/E E/B B♭9♯11 Asus F+/E♭ N.C.
dif - f'rent phrase: _ My new phi - los - o - phy!
ff
Em Em(maj7) C9 N.C.
Some phi - los - o - phies are sim - ple: "Man does not live by bread a - lone." _
mf
8vb
Em Em(maj7) C9
Some phi - los - o - phies are clear: "Leave your mes - sage at the
C7♯5 Fm Fm(maj7)
sound of the tone." _ Some phi - los - o - phies pick and choose _

Fm7 B♭ Gdim7 Am G/B C6
De-cid - ing what goes in it. Some take a life-time, mine take a
sfz
8vb
C♯dim7 D G7 N.C.
min - ute.
Spoken: Schroeder says, "Anything that takes only a minute can't be very lasting. For instance, Beethoven took over two years to complete his brilliant Ninth Symphony." (beat)
I can't stand it. (beat) I can't stand it? I like it!
VAMP
mp
f
Stride-time!
G7
It's like a guar-an - tee, my new phi - los - o - phy,
G Am7 A♯dim7 G/B Cmaj7
and things are sure to be a whole lot bright - er.
Spoken (trying out her new philosophies): Oh yeah,

Cm7
Bm7
E7sus
E♭9
that's what you think!
Why are you telling me?
No!
I can't stand it!
Now life is
mf
G/D
G/E♭
E7
A
Bm7
Cdim7
A/C♯
free and eas - y,
much more phi - los - o - phy - zy,
With my brand new,
8vb
short ending
C/D
N.C.
my new phi - los - o - phy. _
8va
sfz
optional long ending
N.C. Gm D
Ddim/F D/F♯
G
Spoken: You know, someone has said that we should live each day as if it were the last day of our life.
Repeat as needed
mp
N.C.
Clearly, some philosophies aren't for all people.
And that's my new phi - los - o - phy. _
8va
sfz
sfz
8vb

NOTHING

from *A Chorus Line*

Music by Marvin Hamlisch
Lyric by Edward Kleban

rall.
the other, and he says: O.K., we're gonna do improvisations. Now, you're on a bobsled
rall.
a tempo
and it's snowing out. And it's cold . . . O.K., go!
a tempo
Ev-'ry-day for a week we would try to
feel the mo - tion, feel the mo - tion

down the hill.
Ev-'ry day for a week we would try to
hear the wind rush, hear the wind rush,
feel the chill.
And I dug right down to the bot-tom of my soul to see
what I had in - side.
Yes, I dug right down to the

bot-tom of my soul and I tried, ___ I tried.
Spoken: Everyone is going: "Woosh... I feel the snow, I feel the cold...the air." And Mr. Karp
turns to me and says: "O.K. Morales, what did you feel?" Sung: And I said, "Noth-ing, __
Vamp under dialogue
I'm feel - ing noth-ing,"_ and he says, "Noth-ing _ could

get a girl trans - ferred!"
They all felt some-thing,
but I felt noth - ing
ex - cept the
feel - ing that this bull - shit was ab - surd!
Spoken: But I said to myself:
"Hey!, it's only the first week. Maybe it's genetic. They don't have bob sleds in San Juan."

8va
Sec - ond week, more ad - vanced and we had to
be a ta - ble, be a sports car...
ice cream cone. Mis-ter Karp, he would say, "Ver-y good, ex -
cept Mo - ra - les. Try, Mo - ra -

- les, all a-lone."
So I dug right down to the
bot-tom of my soul to see how an ice cream felt.
Yes, I dug right down to the
bot-tom of my soul and I tried to melt.
The kids yelled "Noth-ing!"
They called me

"Noth-ing!" And Karp al - lowed it, which real - ly makes me
burn. They were so help - ful. They called me
hope - less. Un - til I real - ly did - n't know where else to
turn! Spoken: And Karp kept saying: "Morales, I think you should transfer to girls' high.

You'll never be an actress Never!" Jesus Christ!
Sung: Went to church praying, "Santa Maria, send me guidance,
send me guidance." On my knees.
Went to church praying, "Santa Maria, help me feel it,

help me feel it. Pret-ty please!" And a
voice from down at the bot-tom of my soul came up to the top of my head. And the
voice from down at the bot-tom of my soul, here is what it
said: "This man is noth-ing! This course is

noth - ing!
If you want some - thing, go
find a bet - ter class.
And when you
find one,
you'll be an act - ress."
And I as - sure you that's what fi - n'lly came to pass.

Ad lib.
Six months lat - er I heard that Karp had died.
And I dug right down to the bot - tom of my soul....
Slowly
and cried,
'cause I felt. . .
L.H.
Tempo I
noth - ing.
p
p

ONE HUNDRED EASY WAYS TO LOSE A MAN

from *Wonderful Town*

Lyrics by Betty Comden and Adolph Green
Music by Leonard Bernstein

(Spoken flatly)
Just leap out, crawl under the car, say it's the gasket, and fix it in two seconds flat with a bobby pin.
rall.
bat your eyes and say, "What a ro - man - tic spot we're in."
rall.
a tempo
That's a good way to lose a man.
He takes you to a base - ball game, you
fz
p
f
a tempo
sit knee to knee.
He says, "The next man up at bat will bunt, you'll see."
Don't
Just say, "Bunt? Are you nuts?! With no outs, two men on base, and a left-handed batter coming up, he'll walk right into a triple play, just like it happened in the fifth game of the World Series in 1923."
rall.
say, "Oooh, what's a bunt? This game's too hard for lit - tle me."
rall.

a tempo
Faster (but light)
That's a sure way to lose a man. A sure, sure, sure, sure
a tempo
way to lose a man, A splen-did way to lose a man. Just throw your
Tempo I
know-ledge in his face, He'll nev-er try for sec-ond base.
(spoken)
(sung)
Nine-ty-eight ways to go. The third way to lose a man: The

life - guard at the beach that all the girl - ies a dore Swims
brave - ly out to save you through the o - cean's roar, Don't say, "Oh, thanks, I would have drowned in
rall.
rall.
Just push his head under water and yell, "Last one in is a rotten egg" and race him back to shore.
a tempo
just one sec - ond more." That's a swell way to lose a man. You've
f
a tempo
fz
p
found your per - fect mate and it's been love from the start. He

rall.
whis - pers, "You're the one to who I give my heart." Don't say, "I love you, too, my dear, let's
rall.
Just say, "I'm afraid you've made a grammatical error. It's not "To who I give my heart," it's "To whom I give my heart." -- You see, with the use of the preposition "to," "who" becomes the indirect object, making the use of "whom" imperative; which I can easily show you by drawing a simple chart."
a tempo
nev - er, nev - er part." That's a fine way to lose a man. A
f a tempo
p
Tempo II (Faster)
fine, fine, fine, fine way to lose a man, A dan - dy way to lose a
Slow and free
man. Just be more well in - formed than he, You'll nev - er

hear "Oh, prom - ise me." Just show him where his gram - mar errs, Then mark your
f with a beat
Tempo I
tow - els "Hers" and "Hers." Yes, girls, you too can lose your man, if you will
f
use Ruth Sher-wood's plan: "One Hun - dred Eas - y Ways To
Lose A Man!"

SARAH FITCHNER

from *Out of My Head*

Music and Lyrics by
Ryan Scott Oliver

E♭/D♭
Fm7/C
B♭
C5/B♭
- face," It's "Stu - pid Bitch - ner" that's the trend. But
C5/B♭
E♭7
D♭(add9)
Cm7
Liz-zie White is sort of nice to me... She loans me
C5/B♭
Csus
pens. And once in the ca - fe - te - ri - a, She says "Sa -
E♭(add6)
B♭/D
E♭/D♭
Fm7/C
- rah? Want my Rees - es?" I say "O - kay," and fall to pie - ces; LIZ-ZIE'S MY

D♭sus2
FRIEND! My best
E♭sus2 F/E♭ B♭/E♭ C/E♭ (N.C.)
friend! So of
Fsus Fsus/E♭ Gm
course I'm so ex-ci-ted that I tell my news to Kim, who tells Sue, who tells Joy, on their
A♭ E♭sus2 B♭sus2/D
way-to-school walk. I guess, word gets back to Liz-zie, and the next day in the hall, She's

(N.C.)
(As Lizzie.)
F7
got this piece of pa-per and she says, "Hey! We must talk...
B♭5 B♭ Cm B♭/D Gm7 Fm E♭sus2
This is a list of my best friends. Ev'-ry girl is on it, That is,
sfz
f
B♭/D Cm Fsus F7 B♭ Cm Ddim Gsus2/E♭ E♭7 C7/E
Ev'-ry girl BUT, There's this one girl? Who's not? An' I'll tell you what:
E♭M7/F E♭sus2 E♭/D♭ Cm7(♭9)
(Back to Sarah.)
Sor-ry, Sa-rah Fitch-ner; Ya did-n't make the cut." Then she,

(N.C.)/A♭
(Socked in the stomach.)
C5/B♭
B♭m7/F
UGH! Right in the gut...
C5/B♭
E♭7 D♭(add9) C m7
Kap-pa Phi, My so - ro - ri - ty. I have this
C5/B♭
Csus
friend: Al-li - son. Fri-day night at Mi-chael's place, She gets wa -
E♭(add6)
B♭/D
E♭/D♭
F m7/C
- sted, Pu-kin' dra - ma, In the bath - room, I play Ma - ma, Stro-kin' her

D♭sus2
hair, Say - in', "Sa - rah's
E♭sus2 F/E♭ B♭/E♭ C/E♭ (N.C.)
there." An - y - way, the
Fsus Fsus/E♭ Gm
next week, there's a keg - ger At Al - li - son's cha - teau, Hear from Jane, Hear from Kate, Hear from
A♭ E♭sus2 B♭sus2/D
Ming, e - ven Ca - mille! Seems like ev'-ry-one's in-vi - ted... That is, Ev'-ry-one but me. So

(N.C.)
F7
I go up to Al-li-son, and I ask her, "What's your deal?" And she's like,
(As Allison)
B♭5 B♭ Cm B♭/D Gm7 Fm E♭sus2
"I made that list with all our friends, And *they* asked to take you off it. Oh, this is
sfz
f
B♭/D Cm Fsus F7 B♭ Cm Ddim Gsus2/E♭ (N.C.)
real-ly hard to say... To - tal - ly fine with me that you're, um, er, that
C7/E E♭M7/F E♭sus2 E♭/D♭
way, But sor - ry Sa - rah Fitch - ner,

Cm7(♭9)
(Back to Sarah.)
(N.C.)/A♭
They're like, not o - kay. And I said, "Wait... Do you think I'm
Jesus Christ! (etc.)
C5/B♭
B♭m7/F
C5/B♭
B♭m7/F
gay????"
C5/B♭
E♭7 D♭(add9) Cm7
C5/B♭
Work - ing girl, Law firm ten - to - six, a pool of friends. Till
Csus
E♭sus2
B♭/D
Peg - gy catch - es Jen - ni - fer work - ing late, Get - ting slop - py with a part -
8va

E♭/D♭
A♭/C
D♭sus2
- ner, Walt Ko - da - pi. E - mails fly,
E♭sus2
F/E♭
B♭/E♭
C/E♭
(N.C.)
And Jen could die! Then
8vb
Fsus
Fsus/E♭
Gm
one by one I watch our friends for - get that she ex - ists: Peg - gy first, Ja - net next, Mc - Ken - zie
loco
A♭
E♭sus2
Fsus
acts like she's not there. Till at last it's on - ly me and Jen - ni - fer at lunch. At

(N.C.)
mp
first it's kind of awk-ward... 'Cuz Peg-gy's star-ing this way... They want me to come o-ver... So
mp
p
pp
F7
cresc.
I get up from my chair,
f
And I shout,
mp
ff
B♭5 B♭ Cm B♭/D Gm7 Fm E♭sus2
"Peg-gy's a bitch. Ja-net's no one's friend. Mc-Ken-zie will for-get you, If you
sfz
f
B♭/D Cm Fsus F7 B♭ Cm Ddim Gsus2/E♭ C7/E
can't help her ca-reer. There's a good rea-son some friends dis-ap-pear, And

E♭M7/F
E♭sus2
E♭/D♭
E♭7/F
E♭sus2
E♭/D♭
you know Sa - rah Fitch - ner,
Loy - al Sa - rah Fitch -
Rit.
B♭/F
E♭sus2
E♭sus2/D♭
opt.
- ner, Your best friend, best friend, best friend Sa - rah Fitch - ner
A tempo
(N.C.)/F
ten.
C5/B♭
will al - ways be here.
mp
mf
B♭m7/A♭
B♭8
Do ya wan - na grab a beer?"
ff

SHY

from *Once Upon a Mattress*

Words by Marshall Barer
Music by Mary Rodgers

poco rit.
I am just as em - bar - rassed as you? And
poco rit.
I can un - der - stand your point of view: I've al - ways been
ten.
ten.
ten.
Moderately fast 4
Shy, I con-fess it, I'm shy! Can't you guess that this
con - fi - dent air is a mask that I wear, 'cause I'm shy?
p
mf

And you may be sure: way down deep I'm de -
mp
mure. Though some peo - ple I know might de - ny it, At
p
bot - tom I'm qui - et and pure! I'm a - ware that it's
wrong to be meek as I am; My chanc - es may pass me by. I pre - tend to be

strong but as weak as I am, All I can do is try. God knows I
try! Though I'm fright-ened and shy
And de-spite the im-pres-sion I give, I con-fess that I'm liv-ing a
Rubato
lie, Be-cause I'm ac-tual-ly ter-ri-bly ti-mid and hor-ri-bly

Moderate 2
shy.
Though a
la - dy may be drip - ping with gla - mour, As
oft - en as not she - 'll stum - ble and stam - mer When
sud - den - ly con - front - ed with ro - mance.
And she's

like - ly to fall on her face When she's
fi - nal - ly face to face with a pair of pants.
Quite oft - en the la - dy's not as
hard to please as she seems. Quite

oft - en she'll set - tle for some - thing less than the man of her
dreams.
I'm go - ing fish - ing for a mate.
mp
mf
I'm gon - na look in ev - 'ry nook.
mf

But how much long - er must I wait
With
bait - ed breath and ho - ok?
And that is
why, Though I'm pain - ful - ly shy, I'm in - sane to know
Più mosso - Charleston beat
Which sir? You, sir Not you, sir. Then who, sir?

Where, sir And when, sir? I could-n't be ten-ser, So
Let's get this done, man. Get on with the fun, man.
I am one man shy.
fp
mf
Jazz 4
f

THE SECRET SERVICE

from *Mr. President*

Words and Music by
Irving Berlin

C7 C7♯5 F Fm6 N.C. G7
stead - y for the kiss he'll plant, the Se - cret Ser - vice makes me
mind up not to say I won't, the Se - cret Ser - vice makes me
Dm7♭5 Dm7/G G7 C6 N.C. C C6
ner - vous and I can't. They're al - ways spy - ing, no de -
ner - vous and I don't. When things look ros - y they get
Dm7 Dm7/G G7 Dm7 Dm7/G G7
ny - ing, they're al - ways peep - ing, gum - shoe creep - ing, pri - vate
nos - ey, they'll say, "There's toot - sie, play - ing foot - sie, ver - y
Cmaj7 C Gm7 C7 C7♯5
eye - ing. When I'm be - gin - ning to give in - ning like a
co - zy." My pulse goes high - er, I'm on fire, shak - ing

F Fm6 N.C. G7 Dm7♭5 Dm7/G G7
maid - en aunt, the Se - cret Ser - vice makes me ner - vous and I
at the knees, the Se - cret Ser - vice makes me ner - vous and I
C6 N.C. Gm7 C9 C7♯5♭9 Fmaj7 F7
can't. I've been ex - posed be - yond con - trol,
freeze. What - ev - er I may do or say,
F6 N.C. Am7 D9 D7♯5♭9 G9 G7♭9 G7 N.C.
just like a gold - fish in a bowl. The Pres-'dent's
will be re - port - ed the next day. When I'm re -
C C6 Dm7 Dm7/G G7 Dm7 Dm7/G
daugh - ter must drink wa - ter, no drink of scotch she might do
port - ed, it's dis - tort - ed, they don't see clear - ly when I'm

G7 Cmaj7 C Gm7
what she had - n't ought - ter. When I'm ig - nit - ed, so ex -
mere - ly be - ing court - ed. When I'm just neck - ing, sim - ply
C7 C7♯5 F Fm6 N.C. G7 Dm7♭5 Dm7/G G7
cit - ed that I start to pant, the Se - cret Ser - vice makes me ner - vous, when my
peck - ing with a Ca - ry Grant, they stand be - hind me to re - mind me who and
C C7 F F♯dim7 D7/F♯ G7
lamps are lit and I say, "This is it," the Se - cret Ser - vice makes me
what I am when I don't give a damn, the Se - cret Ser - vice makes me
Dm7/G G7 1 C6 N.C. 2 C6
[mf]
ner - vous and I can't. 2. The Se - cret
ner - vous and I can't.
col 8vb

SHOW OFF

from *The Drowsy Chaperone*

Words and Music by Lisa Lambert
and Greg Morrison

Janet is joined by chorus in this number, edited here as a solo.

this no more
play the sauc - y Swiss miss no more
blow my sig - na-ture (kiss) no more.
I don't wan - na show
off.
Don't try to con - trol me
I've made up my mind
And that's
mf
6
3
3

it I quit I'm leav - ing it all be - hind
I don't wan - na be
cute no more Make the gen - tle - men hoot no more.
I don't wan - na wear fruit no more. I don't wan - na show

off.
I don't wan - na show off no more Not
me! read my name in the news no more,
get the glow - ing re -
views no more, Ah gee! I don't wan - na show off!
I don't want to show off!
f
mf
p
cresc.

Wheee! Please no more at - ten - tion
I've count - ed to ten
and I'm
thru. A - dieu You'll nev - er see this...
(she dances)
You'll

(she dances again)
nev - er see this...
(teasing)
Nev - er see this, nev - er see that, ne - ver see these a -
rall.
gain.
Pullback tempo
I don't wan - na change keys no more,
gliss.
accel.
I don't wan - na strip - tease no more. I don't wan - na say

a tempo
cheese no more. I don't care if you scoff
gliss.
3
a tempo
3
I don't wan - na be cheered no more
praised no more
grabbed no more
touched no more
loved no more
I don't wan - na show
off
f
I don't wan - na show off.

I don't wan - na show off.
I don't wan - na show
Faster
off!
ff
no more!

SOMEONE'S BEEN SENDING ME FLOWERS

from *The Shoestring Review*

Words by Sheldon Harnick
Music by David Baker

Am7 D9 G7 C G9 C Dm7 G7
"Thank you" to. Some-times they're thrown through my win - dow or
pa - pier ma - ché. There fol - lowed a gar - land of fun - gus and
C Dm7 G9 C C7 Fmaj7 Em7
down through my chim - ney they fall. Some-times at night when I've
then as a trop - i - cal treat, He sent me a plant that pro -
mf
Dm7 Em7 A7 Dm A+ Dm7 G7 C
turned out my light they come through a crack in the wall.
ceed - ed to pant and lat - er be - gan to eat meat. The
mp
Gm7 C9 Fmaj9 Gm7 C9 Fmaj7
Now that my house is a gar - den, burst-ing with blos-som and bloom,
cac - tus cor - sage touched me deep - ly, A beau - ti - ful plant in its prime.

To Coda
F6 Bm7(♭5) E7 Bm7(♭5) E7 Am7(♭5)
I stand there for hours ad - mir - ing my flowers; I'd like to lie
I felt much the same when the rock gar - den
D7 Am D7 G7 C G9 C
down but there just is - n't room. SOME-ONE'S BEEN SEND-ING ME FLOW-ERS,
mp
Dm7 G7 C Dm7 G9 C C7 Fmaj7
More than I ev - er have had. Re - mark - a - ble
mf
Em7 Dm7 Em7 A7 Dm A+ Dm7 F6 Em7 D7
stuff but e - nough is e - nough. If I see an - oth - er bou - quet,

Slowly, ad lib.
Dm7/G (Tacet)
(spoken) I'll go mad.
C Dm7 G7(♭9) C F
Flow-ers are the lan-guage of love, I'm told,
rall.
sfz
mp
colla voce
C Dm7 C Fmaj7 G7 C Dm7 G7(♭9) C F
a lan-guage di - vine. Ev-'ry dain-ty lit - tle blos-som has a mes-sage to un-fold,
Am7 D7 G D7 G D7
All ex - cept mine. If flow - ers are the lan - guage of af -
D.S. 𝄋 al Coda
G6 G♯m7(♭5) G♯dim Am7 D7 Dm7 G7
fec - tion, how can I in - ter - pret my col - lec - tion? He
rall.
mp

Coda
E7 Am7(♭5) D7 Dm7/G G7
came, one rock at a time.
mp
C G9 C Dm7 G7 C Dm7 G9 C
Some-bod - y mad - ly a - dores me. I know not whom to sus - pect.
C7 Fmaj7 Em7 Dm7 Em7 A7 Dm A+ Dm7
Since I can - not af - ford to be mad - ly a - dored, I do wish you'd
mf
mp
F6 Em7 D7 Dm7 G7 C
stop send-ing flow - ers Col - lect!
mf cresc. poco a poco
ff
sfz
8vb

SPECIAL

from the Broadway Musical *Avenue Q*

Music and Lyrics by Robert Lopez
and Jeff Marx

*Possible cut to ** for auditions.

N.C.
Ebmaj9
Bbm/Db
Gm/D
Cm7
F7b9
F+
(spoken:) Yeah, they're real.
Bbmaj9
Dm7
Ab/Bb
Ebmaj7
When we're to - geth - er, the earth
straight eighths
A7#5
Dm7
will shake, and the stars will fall in - to the
G
Am7
Gdim/Bb
G/B
Cm7
sea. So come on, ba - by, let down

A♭9
your guard.
Dm7
When your date's in the bath - room,
Dm7♭5
I'll
G
Am7
Gdim/B♭
G/B
slip you my card.
I can
Cm7
tell just by
Dm7
look - ing that
E♭maj7
you've got it hard
E♭m/F
N.C.
for
8va
rit.

B♭ B♭/A♭ Gm7♭5 G♭(♭5) F+ B♭7 B♭7/A♭
me! For me!
a tempo
Gm7♭5 G♭(♭5) F+ B♭7 B♭/A♭
For me! For me! For
Gm7♭5 G♭maj7 F7♯5(♯9) N.C.
me! For me! I can tell just by look - in' that you are es - pe - cial - ly
F7♯5(♯9) B♭13
hard for me!
8va
colla voce
8vb

STEPSISTERS' LAMENT

from *Cinderella*

Lyrics by Oscar Hammerstein II
Music by Richard Rodgers

In the show this song is sung by both sisters.

Dm7 G7 Dm G7 C(add2) C Cmaj7/G C6
bub - ble with a flim-sy kind of charm, And with ver-y lit-tle
Am7 D9/A B7 Em G7♯9 G7
trou - ble I could break her lit-tle arm! Oh, oh,
C F Dm7 C/G G13 G7
why would a fel-low want a girl like her, So ob-vious-ly un - u - sual?
C F Dm7 C/E G7 C
Why can't a fel-low ev-er once pre-fer a u-sual girl like me? Her

F C F Adim7/E C
cheeks are a pret-ty shade of pink, But not an-y pink-er than a rose is. Her
F C Am D7 G7#9 G7 C7
skin may be del-i-cate and soft, But not an-y soft-er than a doe's is. Her
F C F Adim7/E C
neck is no whit-er than a swan's. She's on-ly as dain-ty as a dai-sy. She's
F C Am D7 G7#11 G7
on-ly as grace-ful as a bird. So why is the fel-low go-ing cra-zy? Oh,

C
F
Dm7
C/G
why would a fel - low want a girl like her, a girl who's mere - ly
G13
G7
C
F
Dm7
love - ly? Why can't a fel - low ev - er once pre - fer a
C
E7/G♯
Am
Dm9
girl who's mere - ly me? What's the mat - ter with the man? What's the mat - ter with the
G13
C
man? What's the mat - ter with the man?

TAYLOR, THE LATTE BOY

Lyrics by Marcy Heisler
Music by Zina Goldrich

D6/A
Bm7
smiles and says, "How are you?" When he smiles and says, "How are you?" I could
Moderate Pop/Folk (♩ = 98)
E7sus C♯7/E♯
a tempo
F♯m7
swear my heart grows wings. So to - day at eight e - lev - en, I de -
a tempo
mf
A7sus
A7
D(add2)
cid - ed I should meet him. I de - cid - ed I should meet him in a
G7
F♯m7
prop - er for - mal way. So to - day at eight e - lev - en as he

A7sus
A7
D(add2)
smiled and said, "How are you?" I said, "Fine. And my name's Car - ol." And he
Bm7
E7
C♯7/E♯
F♯m7
soft - ly an - swered, "Hey." And I told him, "My name's Car - rol, and
A/E
D♯m7♭5
thank you for the ex - tra foam."
Dm9
G9
A/E
And he said his name was Tay - lor which pro -

*pronounced "pome"

B♭(add2)
E♭(add2)/B♭
like to get my nerve up and re-cite my po-em mu-si-cal. He would
Cm7
E♭/F
B♭sus2
E♭/F
like the fact it's mu-si-cal be-cause he plays gui-tar. And to-
B♭(add2)
E♭(add2)/B♭
day at eight e-lev-en Tay-lor told me he was play-ing with a
Cm7
F7
D7/F♯
band down in the vil-lage in the base-ment of a bar. And he

Gm7 Fm/B♭ B♭7
smooth-ly flipped the lev - er to pre-pare my dou - ble lat - te, but for
E♭ A♭7
me he made it tri - ple, and he did - n't think I knew. But I
Gm7 Fm/B♭ B♭7
saw him flip the lev - er, and for me he made it tri - ple. And I
E♭ Cm7 F7 D7/F♯
knew that tri - ple lat - te meant that Tay-lor loved me, too. I said,

Gm
Gm9/F
"What time are you playing? And thank you for the extra skim."
Em7♭5
E♭m9
A♭9
B♭/F
He said, "Keep the three fifty-five," be-
mf
E♭/F
B♭(add2)
cause this triple latte was on him.
B♭
D7
E♭(add2)
E♭
B♭/D
Taylor the latte boy.
f

Cm7 B♭/D E♭ F7sus D7/F♯ Gm Dm7/F
Bring me ja - va, bring me joy. Oh, Tay - lor, the
C7/E B♭(add2)/F E♭(add2)/F Cm7/B♭ B♭
lat - te boy. I love him. I love him. I love him.
C/D D7♭9 Gm(add2) Gm7 C7sus C7
I used to be the kind of girl who'd run when a love rushed toward
F(add2) F F/E♭ C/D D7♭9 Gm Gm7
'er. But fi - nal - ly a voice whis - pered love can be yours if you

C9sus C9 Cm7 F9 B♭ D7
rit.
a tempo
step up to the coun - ter and or der... Tay - lor, the
rit.
ff a tempo
E♭(add2) E♭ B♭/D Cm7 B♭/D E♭ F7sus D7/F♯
lat - te boy. Bring me ja - va, bring me joy. Oh Tay -
f
Gm Dm7/F C7/E B♭(add2)/F E♭(add2)/F
- lor, the lat - te boy. I love him. I love him. I love
Cm7/B♭ B♭ E♭maj7 Cm/E♭ F5/D B♭/D
him. So man - y years my heart has wait - ed.
f

D7 C/E D7/F♯ Gm7 C9 Cm7♭5/G♭
Who'd have thought that love could be so caf - fein - at - ed.
B♭/F D7/F♯ Gm7 C9
Tay - lor, the lat - te boy. I
ff
B♭(add2)/F E♭(add2)/F D7/F♯ Gm7 C9
love him. I love him. I love him. I
B♭/F rit. E♭/F Cm7/B♭ B♭(add2)
love him. I love him. I love him.
mf rit.

THAT DIRTY OLD MAN

from *A Funny Thing Happened on the Way to the Forum*

Words and Music by
Stephen Sondheim

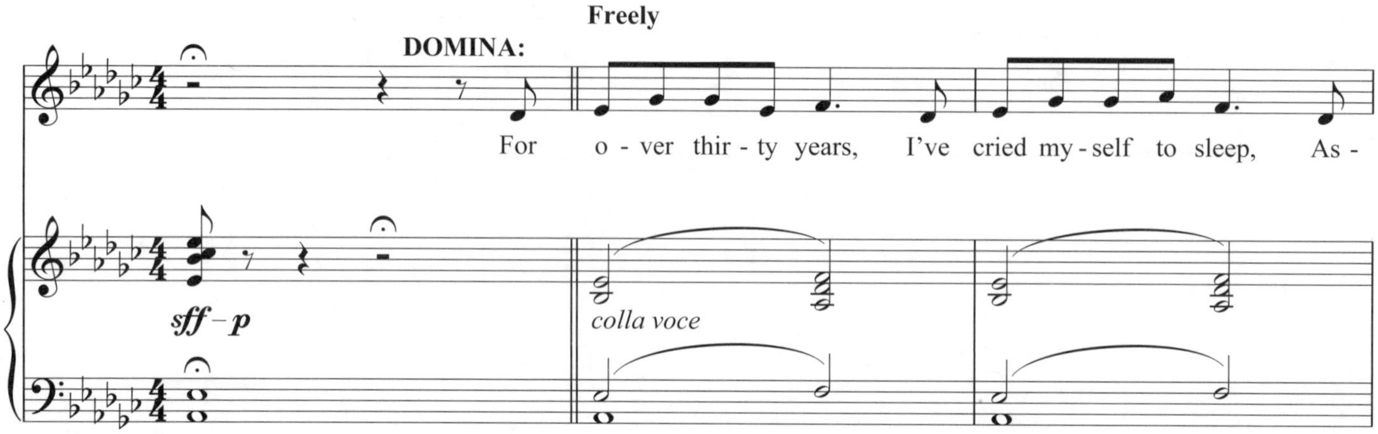

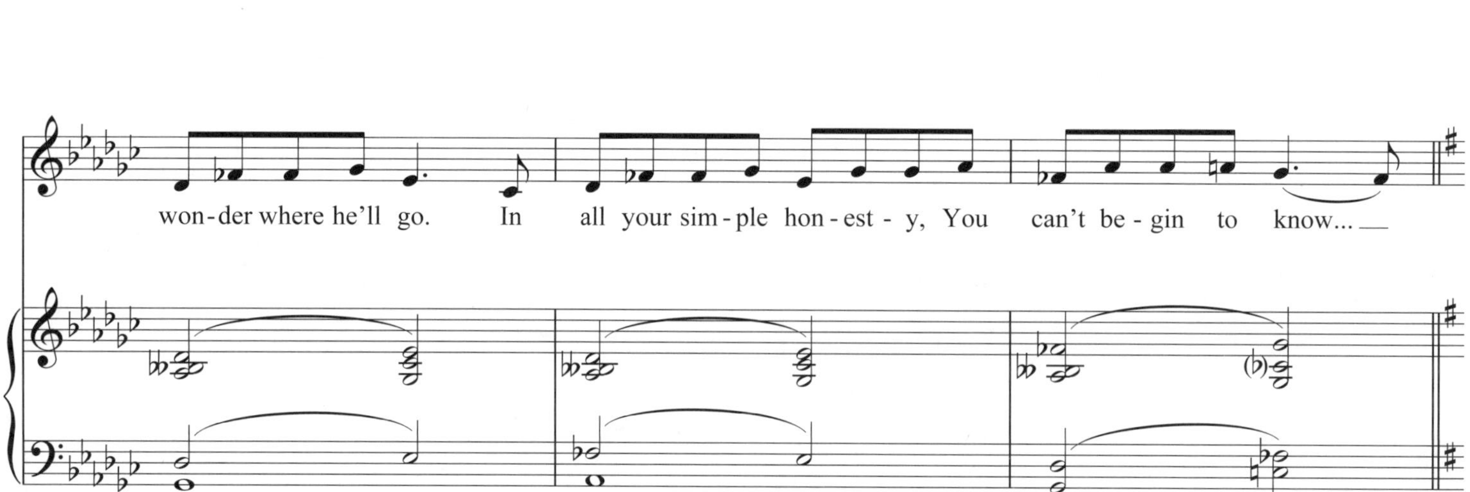

(wail)
Ohhh...
I want him, I
need him. Where is
Con fuoco
he? That dir - ty old man is here some - where, Ca -
mf

vort - ing with some - one young and fair, Dis - port - ing in ev - 'ry shame - less whim, Just
wait till I get my hands on him—! I'll hold
him, En - fold him. Where
is he? That

dir - ty old man, where can he be? Pro - fan - ing our vows for all to see, Com -
plain - ing how he's mis - un - der - stood, A - bus - ing me (if he on - ly would!)... Oh,
love, Sweet love, Why hide? You
ver - min, you worm, you vil - lain! Come face, Em - brace Your

bride! Where - ev - er he is, I know he's still an
an - gel. My an -
gel! Where is he, That
dir - ty old man di - vine? I love

him, I love him! That
poco rall.
lech-er-ous, lewd, las-civ - i-ous, Loath-some, ly-ing, la-zy, Dir - ty old man of
poco rall.
colla voce
[a tempo]
mine!
3
3
f [a tempo]
fz

THAT'LL SHOW HIM

from *A Funny Thing Happened on the Way to the Forum*

Music and Lyrics by
Stephen Sondheim

Our re - venge will start!
When I kiss him, I'll be kiss - ing you,
So I'll kiss him morn - ing and night—! That - 'll show him!
When I hold him, I'll behold - ing you,
So I'llhold him

ten times as tight—! That - 'll show him, too!
I shall coo, and ten - der - ly stroke his
hair. Wish that you were there—
You'd en - joy it! When it's eve - ning And we're in our
mp
p
3

tent for two, I'll sit on his knee,
Get to know him In - ti - mate - ly— That - 'll show him
How much I real - ly love you!
f
f

TO KEEP MY LOVE ALIVE

from *A Connecticut Yankee*

Music by Richard Rodgers
Lyrics by Lorenz Hart

[rit.]
Yet, re - mem - ber these sweet words, "Till death do us part."
[rit.]
REFRAIN
With care and elegance and rubato
I mar - ried man - y men, a ton of them, be - cause I was un - true to none of them, be - cause I bumped off ev - 'ry one of them to keep my love a - live. Sir
thought Sir George had pos - si - bil - i - ties, but his flir - ta - tions made me ill at ease, and when I'm ill at ease, I kill at ease to keep my love a - live. Sir
p

Paul was frail, he looked a wreck to me. At night he was a hor - se's
Charles came from a san - a - to - ri - um, and yelled for drinks in my em -
neck to me, so I per-formed an ap - pen - dec - to - my, to
po - ri - um. I mixed one drink, he's in me - mo - ri - am, to
keep my love a - live! Sir Tho - mas had in - som - ni - a, he
keep my love a - live! Sir Fran - cis was a sing - ing bird, a
could-n't sleep at night, I bought a lit - tle ar - sen - ic, he's
night - in - gale, That's why I tossed him off my bal - co - ny to
mf

sleep ing now all right. Sir Phil-ip played the harp, I cussed the thing. I
see if he could fly. Sir Ath-el-stane in-dulged in frat-ri-cide, he
crowned him with his harp to bust the thing, and now he plays where harps are
killed his dad and that was pat-ri-cide. One night I stabbed him by my
just the thing, to keep my love a-live, to keep my love a-
mat-tress side, to keep my love a-live, to
1
ten.
a tempo
live. I keep my love a-live.
2
opt.
sf

A TRIP TO THE LIBRARY

from *She Loves Me*

Words by Sheldon Harnick
Music by Jerry Bock

MISS RITTER: *(Spoken before the introduction) Let me tell you, you've never seen anything like that library. So many books. . . so much marble. . . so quiet!*

Bolero

start-ed to reach for a book and my hand aut-o-mat-i-c'lly came to a stop. I
don't know how long I stood fro-zen, a vic-tim of pan-ic and mor-ti-fi-ca-tion.
With Freedom
Oh, how I want-ed to flee when a kind-ly voice, a
rall.
Moderato
gen-tle voice whis-pered "Par-don me."
rall.

And there _ was this dear, sweet, clear-ly re - spec - ta - ble thick-ly be - spec - ta-cled
man who stood _ by my side and qui - et - ly said _ to me "Ma'am,
Don't mean _ to in - trude, but I was just won - der-ing are you in need _ of some
help?" I said "no . . . Yes, I am!"
mf
(mf)

The next thing I know I'm sip-ping hot choc-'late and
tell-ing my trou-bles to Paul, whose ten-der brown eyes kept send-ing com-pas-sion-ate
looks. A trip to the li-brar-y has made a new
girl of me, for sud-den-ly I can see the mag-ic of

books.
I
p
have to ad-mit in the back of my mind, I was pray-ing he would-n't get fresh.
And
sim.
all of the while I was won-der-ing why an il - lit - er-ate girl should at - tract him.
Then
all of a sud-den he said that I could-n't go wrong with "The Way of All Flesh."
Of

course, it's a nov-el, but I did-n't know or I cer-tain-ly would-n't have smacked him. Well, he gave me a
smile, that I could-n't re - sist, and I knew at once how
rall.
Moderato
much I liked this op - tom - e - trist.
mf
You know what this dear, sweet, slight-ly be - spec - ta-cled gen-tle-man said to me

next? He said he could solve this prob-lem of mine. I said "How?"
He said if I'd like he'd will-ing-ly read to me some of his fa - vor-ite
things. I said "When?" He said "Now." His nov - el ap -
p
f
proach seemed high-ly sus - pi - cious and pos - si - bly dan - ger-ous too. I told my-self

wait, think, dare you go up to his flat. What hap - pens if
things go wrong? It's ob - vi-ous he's quite strong. He read to me
rall.
Rubato
Deliberately
all night long, now how - a-bout that! It's hard to be - lieve how
rall.
pp
tru-ly do-mes - tic and hap-pi-ly hope - ful I feel. I pic - ture my Paul there

reading aloud as I cook.
As long as he's there to read there's quite a good
chance indeed, a chance that I'll never need to open a
book!
Rubato
Unlike someone else someone I dimly recall.
a tempo
I know he'll only have eyes for me, my optometrist Paul.
sfz

WHATEVER HAPPENED TO MY PART?

from *Monty Python's Spamalot*

Lyrics by Eric Idle
Music by John Du Prez and Eric Idle

G A/G D(add2)/F♯ D/F♯ F(add2) G/F
stage for far too long. It's ag - es since I had a
C(add2)/E C/E Em7 A7
song. This is one un - hap - py di - va. The pro -
Em7 A Em Em7/D
duc - ers have de - ceived her. There is noth - ing I can sing from my
A/C♯ A A/C♯ C D6 D7 G/D D G
heart. What-ev - er hap-pened to my part? I am

Em7
D/F♯
sick of my ca-reer al-ways stuck in sec-ond gear, up to
detached
G Asus A D(add2)
C♯m7 F♯7sus F♯/A♯
here with frus-tra-tion and with fears. I've no Gram-my, no re-wards. I've no
Bm Bm/A Em7 Asus A
To-ny A-wards. I'm con-stant-ly re-placed by Brit-ney Spears. Brit-ney
p
cresc.
B♭m7/E♭ E♭7 A♭ Gm7♭5 C7
rall.
a tempo
Spears! What-ev-er hap-pened to my
cresc.
rall.
mf a tempo

Fm Ab7/Eb Db Cm7b5 F7/A Bbm Bbm/Ab
show? I was a hit. Now, I don't know. I'm with a
mp
Gb Db/F Ebm7 Absus Ab B/Db Db
bunch of Brit-ish knights, pran-cing 'round in wool - y tights! I mightas
cresc.
F# G#/F# C#(add2)/F C#/F E(add2) F#/E
well go to the pub. They've been out search - ing for a
f
B(add2)/D# B/D# D#m7 G# D#m6 G#
shrub. Out shop-ping for a bush! Well, they can kiss my tush! It

D♯m D♯m/C♯ G♯/B♯ G♯
seems to me they've real - ly lost the plot.
cresc.
B C♯ B C♯ B C♯
molto rit.
What-ev - er hap-pened to my— I'll call my a - gent, dam - mit— what-ev - er hap-pened to my...
ff
molto rit.
Freely
N.C.
Broadly
F♯
not yours... not yours... but my part?
B/F♯ molto rit. C♯/F♯ F♯
molto rit.

WAITING

from *The Addams Family*

Music and Lyrics by
Andrew Lippa

Growing in intensity
Dm7 G Dm7 G
waits for her big Mal to come back home at
Dm7 G Dm7 G Dm7 G
five o'-clock, or six o'-clock, 'til it's nine o'-clock! And there's
cresc. poco a poco
Dm7 G Dm7 G E7sus♭9
rit.
no o'-clock ___ to ease the pain, pain she can't ex - plain. As the wom-an
f
rit.
Expressive and expansive, à la French chanteuse
Cmaj7 Cmaj7♯5 Cmaj7/G C/F♯ F9♯11
waits in the dark for a spark that once was there that is - n't
mp
cresc. poco a poco

Grand
Bbmaj7
molto rit.
Dm(add2)
A/C#
Am/C
there, not ev - er there!
molto rit.
ff
F/G
G9
molto rit.
Ab/C
poco accel.
Fm6/C
Abmaj7/C
Fm6/9/C
Abmaj7/C
A - lone and wait - ing and wail - ing, whin - ing and wan - ing, want - ing and
p sub. molto rit.
poco accel.
Ab(add#4)/C
Fm(add2)/C
Fm6/C
accel. e cresc. poco a poco
Ab(add2)/C
Bb(add2)/C
Ab(add2)/C
wast - ing and woe. Wait - ing, fix - at - ing, de - bat - ing, lose
accel. e cresc. poco a poco
Bb(add2)/C
Fm6/C
Ab/C
molto rit.
C7sus
rit.
Ebm6
weight - ing, ice skat - ing, lac - tat - ing. And so we wait to
molto rit.
rit.

Sweetly
B♭maj7/F
Gm7/F
F7(add4)
E♭(add2)/F
laugh, we wait to cry, we wait for ev - 'ry hope - ful
p
8va
G♭7♭5
E♭(add2)/F
E♭(add♯4)/F
C♯m7/F
F(add♭6)
breath. Wait - ing for a lous - y, rot - ting, vi - cious, ran - cid,
cresc. poco a poco
Horror Movie
F13
F7(add4)
F9♯11
F♯m/F
B♭m
E♭9/B♭
rit.
flushed-down, fet - id, fren - zied, fa - tal death!
ff
C♭/C
C♭(♭5)
B♭m7(add11)
molto rit.
sffz
8vb

WHEN YOU GOT IT, FLAUNT IT

from *The Producers*

Music and Lyrics by
Mel Brooks

Ulla sings this song with a Swedish accent in the show.

F6/C
G9/D
C7
got it,
flaunt it.
Show your as - sets let 'em know you're
mp
Em7 A7
D9
G13
proud.
Your
good - ies you must push, stick your
chest out, shake your tush, ven you
Cool Swing
F6/C G9/C C7♭9
F6 Gm7/C F6/9
F
got it, shout _ it out
loud! ____
Ven you got it
mf
mp
G
C7
F6 F♯dim7 C13
show it
put your hid - den trea - sures on dis - play

F6/9 Gm7 C9 Gm9 C11
Vi - o - lin - ists love to play an E - string But au - di - enc - es real - ly love a
F/A G♯dim7 Gm7 C13 F6 G7
G - string Ven you got it, shout it.
mf
C7 A7 D7
Let the whole vorld hear vat you're a - bout Clothes may make the man, all a
G7 Gm9 D♭7♯5 C13 F6
girl needs is a tan ven you got it let it hang out. Ven

Sweetly
straight 8ths
Em7b5 A7 Dm A7b9 Dm Em7b5 A7
I was yust a lit - tle girl in Sve - den my thought-ful mo - ther gave me this ad -
mp
Dm Dm7 G7 C6 Am7
vice: If na - ture bles - ses you from top to bot - tom,
8va
Swing!
Dm11 G13 C13
show that top to bot - tom, don't think twice. Don't think
mf
Abm9/Db Db13 Abm/Db Bbm/Cb Cb/Bb Db/Ab
twice. Ven you
f

Broad swing
G6 G6/F♯ Em7 G6/D A13 A13/G A13/F♯ A13/E
got it ___ share it. ___
ff
D7 D9 G6 E7/G♯ Am7 D9
Let the pub - lic feast up - on your charms.
G G/F♯ Em7 G/D Am11 D7 Am11 D13
Peo - ple say that be - ing prim is prop - er, ___ But ev - 'ry show - girl knows that "prim" will
mf
G E♭9 A♭ A♭/G Fm9 A♭/E♭
stop her. ___ Ven you got it, ___
f

B♭7
give it.
E♭7
Don't be self - ish, give it all a -
B♭m/D♭
C7
B♭add9/D
vay!
E♭dim7
C7/E
Don't be
F7
shy, be bold and cute,
show the
B♭9♭5
boys that birth - day suit
ven you
p
ff

"Going home"
Bbm9
Dbm7
got it
If you got it
Ab6/Eb
Bb9/Eb
Eb13
Once you got it
shout out hoo -
gliss.
Samba-straight 8ths
Eb7
Ab
ray!
Ab/Gb
Db/F
Dbm/Fb
Eb7sus
Ab6/9